SWAMP THINGS

Animal Life in a Wetland

Cottonmouth

by Ellen Lawrence

Consultant:

Stephen Hammack
Herpetarium Keeper
St. Louis Zoo
St. Louis, Missouri

BEARPORT
PUBLISHING

New York, New York

Credits

Cover, © Byron Jorjorian/Alamy; 4, © Jo Crebbin/Shutterstock; 5, © ABN Images/Alamy; 7, © Pierson Hill; 8, © Pete Oxford/Minden Pictures/FLPA; 9, © Ivan Kuzmin/Alamy; 9R, © Alissala Kerr/Shutterstock; 10, © Coy St. Clair/Shutterstock; 11, © Don Mammoser/Shutterstock; 11B, © imageBROKER/Alamy; 12, © Rob Hainer/Shutterstock; 13, © Paul S. Wolf/Shutterstock; 14, © Paul S. Wolf/Shutterstock; 15, © Paul S. Wolf/Shutterstock; 16, © Robert Hamilton/Alamy; 17, © Alan Cressler; 18, © Karl H. Switak/Ardea; 19, © Rolf Nussbaumer/Nature Picture Library; 20, © Byron Jorjorian/Alamy; 21, © Karl H. Switak/Ardea; 22T, © Ruby Tuesday Books; 22B, © Watcher Fox/Shutterstock; 23TL, © Photo Researchers/FLPA; 23TC, © Jo Crebbin/Shutterstock; 23TR, © Stubblefield Photography/Shutterstock; 23BL, © FlavoredPixels/Shutterstock; 23BC, © Gerald A. DeBoer/Shutterstock; 23BR, © Martha Marks/Shutterstock.

Publisher: Kenn Goin
Editor: Jessica Rudolph
Creative Director: Spencer Brinker
Design: Emma Randall
Photo Researcher: Ruby Tuesday Books Ltd

Library of Congress Cataloging-in-Publication Data

Names: Lawrence, Ellen, 1967– , author.
Title: Cottonmouth / by Ellen Lawrence.
Description: New York, New York : Bearport Publishing, 2017. | Series: Swamp things : animal life in a wetland | Includes bibliographical references and index.
Identifiers: LCCN 2016016138 (print) | LCCN 2016024914 (ebook) | ISBN 9781944102524 (library binding) | ISBN 9781944997182 (ebook)
Subjects: LCSH: Agkistrodon piscivorus—Juvenile literature.
Classification: LCC QL666.O69 L39 2017 (print) | LCC QL666.O69 (ebook) | DDC 597.96—dc23
LC record available at https://lccn.loc.gov/2016016138

For more information, write to Bearport Publishing Company, Inc., 45 West 21st Street, Suite 3B, New York, New York 10010. Printed in the United States of America.

10 9 8 7 6 5 4 3 2 1

Contents

A Swimming Snake

It's dawn in the Florida Everglades.

A cottonmouth snake is swimming across a pond.

The snake has spent the night hunting in the water.

Now it slithers out of the pond and curls up on a log.

The cottonmouth warms up in the early morning sunshine.

a cottonmouth swimming

Snakes are **reptiles**, which are cold-blooded animals. A reptile's body temperature changes with the temperature of its surroundings.

a cottonmouth warming up in the sun

A Cottonmouth's World

Cottonmouths live in **wetlands,** such as the Everglades.

In some parts of the Everglades, tough grasses grow from the wet ground.

In other areas, there are swamps, where trees and bushes grow from the water-covered land.

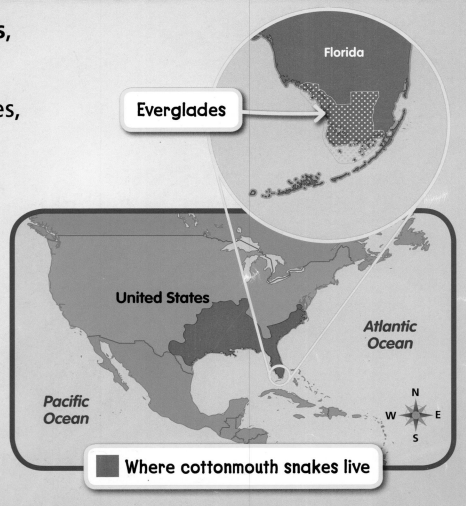

Florida

Everglades

United States

Atlantic Ocean

Pacific Ocean

N
W E
S

Where cottonmouth snakes live

Cottonmouths that live in cool areas **hibernate** in tree stumps during the cold winter months. In warmer areas, like Florida, cottonmouths don't hibernate.

a swamp in the Everglades

How do you think cottonmouths got their name?

cottonmouth

Meet a Cottonmouth

A cottonmouth has a thick, scaly body and a wide, flat head.

A young cottonmouth may have light-colored scales and a banded pattern on its body.

As the snake grows older, its scales turn dark brown or black, and it loses its pattern.

Cottonmouths can grow up to 4 feet (1.2 m) long and weigh 3 pounds (1.4 kg).

scaly skin

Danger in the Swamp

A cottonmouth shares its swampy home with animals that may try to eat it!

When a large bird or other **predator** comes near, the snake tries to defend itself.

The cottonmouth coils its body and raises up its head.

Then it opens its mouth wide.

This warns predators: *Don't mess with me!*

How do you think a cottonmouth catches its food?

great horned owl

Cottonmouths are sometimes eaten by alligators, snapping turtles, and larger snakes. Birds such as owls and eagles also hunt the snakes.

snapping turtle

On the Hunt!

A cottonmouth hunts for small animals in water and on land. How?

The snake has a small hole, called a pit, on each side of its head.

These pits can sense heat coming from an animal's body.

When an animal gets close, the cottonmouth senses its body heat and strikes!

Then the snake bites its victim with its fangs.

pit

A cottonmouth's fangs are hollow like drinking straws. When the snake bites an animal, **venom** shoots down the fangs into the animal.

a cottonmouth biting a bullfrog

Hungry Snakes

After a cottonmouth bites an animal, it doesn't start eating right away.

First it checks to make sure the venom has killed its victim.

The cottonmouth does this by touching the animal with its long, forked tongue.

Then the snake swallows the dead animal whole, head first!

Cottonmouths mostly hunt fish, frogs, and toads. Sometimes they eat mice, small turtles, baby alligators, and bird eggs.

forked tongue

dead bullfrog

a cottonmouth
swallowing a bullfrog

15

Baby Cottonmouths

In spring, male and female cottonmouths meet up to **mate**.

About four months later, the female snake finds a safe place to give birth, such as under a log.

There, she has up to 20 babies.

Soon after the baby snakes are born, they slither away from their mother.

They are just a few hours old, but they can take care of themselves!

baby cottonmouth

yellow tip

A baby cottonmouth has a tail with a yellow tip, which it uses to catch food. How do you think it does this?

Baby cottonmouths have a pattern of brown and orange bands. This pattern helps the babies blend in with plants and rocks so they can hide from predators.

Little Hunters

After leaving its mother, a baby cottonmouth goes hunting.

It wriggles the tip of its tail from side to side.

Small frogs and fish think the snake's tail is a tasty worm.

Once an animal gets close, the baby snake bites it.

As a cottonmouth grows older, the tip of its tail becomes brown or black.

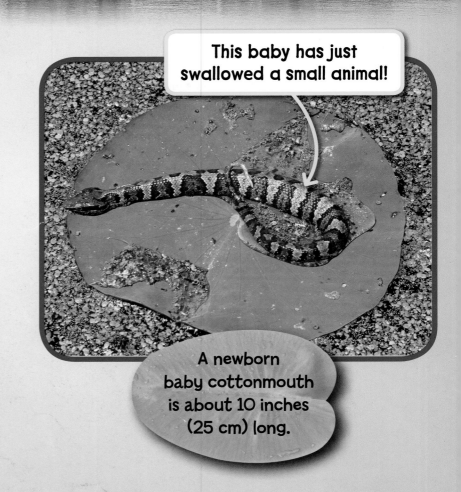

This baby has just swallowed a small animal!

A newborn baby cottonmouth is about 10 inches (25 cm) long.

a baby cottonmouth
hunting on a lily pad

Growing Bigger

As a cottonmouth grows bigger, its scaly skin gets too tight.

Every few months, it sheds— or wriggles out of—its old skin.

Underneath the old skin is shiny new skin.

It takes about three years for a cottonmouth to be fully grown.

Then the snake is ready for its grown-up life—swimming and hunting in the swamp.

adult cottonmouth

old skin

new skin

An adult cottonmouth sheds its skin several times each year.

Science Lab

Blending In

Imagine you are a scientist who studies cottonmouths. Make a model of a baby cottonmouth to investigate how its skin color and patterns help it to blend into different surroundings.

Do you think it will be difficult or easy to see the snake model when you place it outdoors?

Write your predictions in your notebook.

1. Using clay, create a model of a baby cottonmouth.

2. Take your model outside. Choose three different places to set it down. For example: on a log, on dry leaves, and on grass.

Is the model easy or difficult to see?
Did your predictions match what you observed?

You will need:
- Brown, orange, and yellow modeling clay
- A notebook and a pencil

Science Words

hibernate (HYE-bur-nayt) to go into a sleeplike state during periods of cold weather

mate (MAYT) to come together to produce young

predator (PRED-uh-tur) an animal that hunts other animals for food

reptiles (REP-tylez) cold-blooded animals that have dry, scaly skin, such as snakes and lizards

venom (VEN-uhm) poison that some animals can send into the bodies of other animals through a bite or sting

wetlands (WET-landz) habitats where most of the land is covered with shallow water and plants

Index

Read More

Gagne, Tammy. *Snakes: Built for the Hunt (First Facts).* North Mankato, MN: Capstone (2016).

Gambino, Karlie. *Cottonmouth (Killer Snakes).* New York: Gareth Stevens (2012).

Lawrence, Ellen. *A Snake's Life (Animal Diaries: Life Cycles).* New York: Bearport (2012).

Learn More Online

To learn more about cottonmouths, visit **www.bearportpublishing.com/SwampThings**

About the Author

Ellen Lawrence lives in the United Kingdom. Her favorite books to write are those about nature and animals. In fact, the first book Ellen bought for herself, when she was six years old, was the story of a gorilla named Patty Cake that was born in New York's Central Park Zoo.